Vision 20/20
Twenty Psalms for the Twentieth Century

Vision 20/20
Twenty Psalms for the Twentieth Century

Sister Rose Agnes MacCauley S.C.

Fides Publishers Inc., Notre Dame, Indiana

©Copyright: 1971, Fides Publishers, Inc., Notre Dame, Indiana

Library of Congress Catalog Card Number: 76-172640

International Standard Book Number: 0-8190-0078-7

Dedication

To my sister, Helen, in whom I have seen exemplified
the philosophy of these psalms: "In God I transcend my hates and fears and
reach out to others in love and trust" (Ps. 16, vv. 2, 3).

Preface

Here are twenty psalms interpreted in the light of a twentieth century Christian's vision. The beauty of the psalms, it seems to me, is somehow diminished if we regard them as static prayer forms. There is a dynamism inherent in them which each generation must make its own. In the psalms, man confronts God openly, giving full expression to his gladness and his grief, his fears, his frustrations, his antipathies, and, through it all, his utter trust in Yahweh. We do injustice to the psalmist, I think, when we suppose that the imprecations which he calls down on his enemies are the full measure of his prayer. It would probably be closer to the truth to suppose that these are the sincere outbursts of a man who talked very honestly to God and, by disclosing his aversions, paved the way for conversion. The process of conversion still goes on as men of every age struggle with their antipathies, their jealousies, their distrust toward their fellowmen. Deep in the heart of the psalmist — and the heart of every man — is Yahweh's answer. Perhaps now is the time to look for ways of articulating this answer.

In the twenty psalms that follow, I have attempted to do something like this. As one who, over a long period of years, has derived inspiration from the psalms, I would like to share with others insights that have had an impact on my own philosophy of living and loving.

In some cases, as in Psalm 12, I have begun with verses from the original psalm, and then attempted a reinterpretation which I have entitled: *Yahweh answers.* In other instances, as in Psalm 3, I have tried to capture the tone of the psalmist as it is reflected or refracted in contemporary situations. The photographs exemplify such situations. As I have indicated in the dedication, the philosophy of these psalms is one of love and trust. To all who read them, I extend this love and trust, and I invite them to join me in understanding worship as "a disposition to grow: to recognize God in the process that moves us onward and upward." *(Psalm 16:4-6)*

Design:
Michael Rider

Photography:
Virginia Belive — page 47
D. R. Goff — pages 15, 17, 19, 35, 39, 45, 49, 55
Justin A. Soleta — pages 13, 21, 23, 25, 29, 31, 33, 43, 51, 57, 59, 61, 63
The New York Times — page 41

Contents

Vision of Love

Vision of Trust

Vision of Concern

Vision of Hope

Vision of Love

"I have loved you with an everlasting love;
therefore I have continued my faithfulness to you."
Je. 31:3

*To be blessed is to say yes when God asks us
to build a better world for others.*

Psalm 1

Blessed is the man who resists every plan
That the wicked devise to destroy others.

Blessed is the man whose law is love . . .
Love for God and all that God has made.

To be blessed is to say yes when God asks us
to build a better world for others.

To be wicked is to trample on others,
Or shrewdly destroy them whenever they get in our way.

The Lord loves the blessed and his love renews their life;
The Lord loves the wicked and invites them to repent,
Even while he censures their deeds;
But the wicked laugh at his love and prefer to rival his power.

By love, you were begotten; by love, you live and grow.

Psalm 2

Why do nations oppose one another and why are people uptight?
Let us break the bonds of distrust that tie us to narrow views,
And hinder us from stretching out our hands and hearts to others.

He who is ever with us says to us:
"You whom I made are my sons;
By love you were begotten;
By love you live and grow.

The earth is yours to possess and share in family affection.
Put down your 'rods of iron' — your nuclear weapons and
deadly devices for destroying life.

Life was given to be lived and loved;
Your life, and the lives of others must advance together
To that point of contact where I am all in all."

Keep rising when you fall, and be decent enough,
when you're on your feet, to help others to rise.

Psalm 15

O Lord, who shall sojourn in your tent?
Who shall dwell on your holy hill?
He who walks blamelessly and does what is right?
But who of us is blameless?
Those who rate themselves such, I see as self-righteous.

Yahweh answers:
"It is not the 'blameless' who delight me.
It is not the self-styled righteous whom I seek.
It is the struggling 'sinner' who isn't afraid to admit he's failed;
Who finds room in his heart to excuse the failures of others.
Remember, my tent is the sanctuary of the Ark of the Covenant,
And only those who subscribe to my Covenant of Love can feel at home there.
My Covenant of Love reads like this:
Be loving enough to say, 'I'm sorry'
when you haven't followed through with me or your fellow men.
Be steadfast enough to translate what you say
into effective measures of reconciliation.
Keep rising when you fall, and be decent enough,
when you're on your feet, to help others to rise.
Thus you will become incorporated in the Saving Act of my Beloved Son.
Thus you will translate into the language of the hour
The words my Son once spoke:
No one has ascended into heaven but he who first descended."

It is not for the destruction of my enemies that I pray,
but for the destruction of enmity.

Psalm 9

I will give thanks to you, Lord, with all my heart;
I will tell of your wonderful deeds,
And because of these deeds, I dare to hope
That the prayer I now make will find fulfillment.

It is not for the destruction of my enemies that I pray,
But for the destruction of enmity.
Root out the canker within us that makes us resist one another.
You are a stronghold, O Lord, to the oppressed.
Let your strength impel us, when we have become strong,
Not to turn the tables on our oppressors.
Help us, rather, by the force of our commitment
To eradicate from the heart of every man
Any desire to exploit his fellow man.
May the needy no longer be forgotten;
May the hope of the poor not perish forever.

continued

Psalm 9

Arise, O Lord. Let man prevail
As you intend that he should.

Let him prevail as the Man for Others,
As the one who has come down that we may rise,
Who has caught us up in the embrace of his love;
Whose plan of battle is to invite foes to be his friends,

Not by surrendering their freedom, but by understanding it
As the acceptance of a dimension that transcends time,

As a response to the purpose that governs our lives —
To reflect love, that "God may be all in all."

One must look, listen, and love,
before one can respond to the call of another.

Psalm 17

The disciple speaks:
Hear, O Lord, a just suit; attend to my outcry;
hearken to my prayer from lips without deceit.
From you let my judgment come;
Your eyes behold what is right.
Though you test my heart, searching it in the night,
though you try me with fire, you shall find no malice in me.
My mouth has not transgressed after the manner of man.
According to the words of your lips I have kept the ways of the law.

Yahweh answers:
I must tell you that I do not like your tone.
It is too self-righteous, too concerned with vindication.
It is not Myself, the God of Love whom you worship;
It is a small god which your small mind has fashioned
A God who rewards and punishes.
You have tried to cut me down to your own size,
To fit me into your system of weights and measurements

Continued

Psalm 17

And in so doing you have stunted your own growth.
You say you have not "transgressed after the manner of man."
You tell me what you have not done,
And I ask, "What *have* you done after the manner of man?"
Have you lived? Have you loved?
Have you plunged into deep waters to rescue the shipwrecked?
You tell me you have kept the ways of the law
Have you tried to understand the ways of the lawless?
Have you opened your eyes to their problems
and opened your heart to their needs?
If you want me to hear, you must speak my language.
It is a very simple language but it takes a lifetime to master.
It is spoken with the eyes, with the ears, with the heart
before the lips utter a sound,
One must look, listen, love,
before one can respond to the call of another.

Vision of Trust

The Lord came to Abram in a vision,
"Fear not Abram, I am your shield."
Gen. 15:1

In you I transcend my hates and fears,
and reach out to others in love and trust.

Psalm 16

Preserve me, O God, for in you I live;
In you, I transcend my hates and fears,
And reach out to others in love and trust.

The worship you ask is a disposition to grow:
To recognize you in the process that moves me onward and upward.

To think of you in static terms is to worship an idol —
And idolatry does violence to God and man.
It reduces divinity to a lifeless image,
And stifles man's yearning for growth and challenge.

I denounce idolatry, Lord;
I refuse to be entrapped in the meshes of a fixed and changeless situation.
In you I find the strength and incentive to question, to probe, to grow;
In you I find the power to transcend myself
and move steadfastly, fearlessly, fervently
toward the Summit — the meeting of God and man.

Psalm 5

Listen to me, Lord, as I cry out to you,
As I greet the new day with prayers for your help,
And praises for your goodness.

I find myself appalled by the evil that prevails,
by the games of treachery and deceit that some seem to enjoy.

I am disheartened when they deride values that I cherish
And when they find only evil reports newsworthy.

You are not this way, O Lord.
You offer your people truth as the way to freedom.

You offer your people love,
And you invite them to trust you and one another.

Let your spirit of truth direct us that we may
be truly free and that we may choose sincerity rather than shrewdness.

Let your spirit of love inspire us that we may find joy in service
and that we may choose sensitivity rather than cynicism.

Let your spirit of trust encompass us that we may
think well of others and that we may choose respect
for life rather than retention of power.

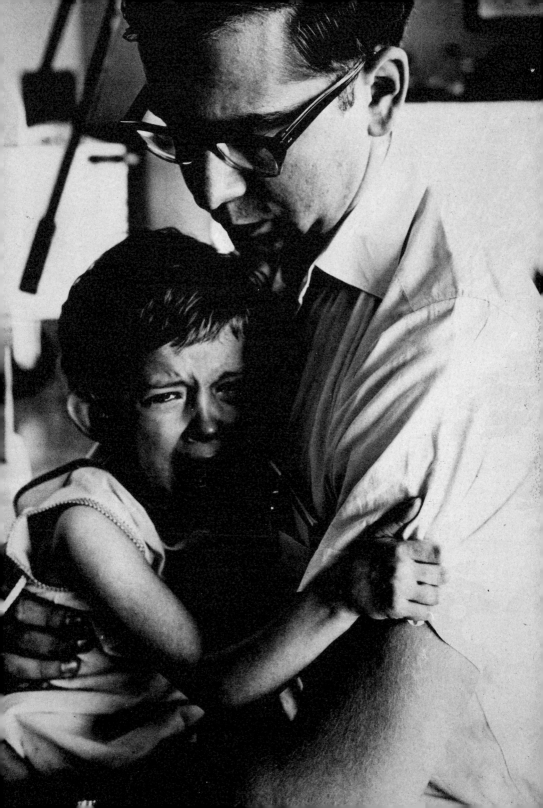

How long, O Lord? Will you forget me forever?

Psalm 13

How long, O Lord? Will you forget me forever?
How long will you hide your face from me?
How long must I bear pain in my soul;
And have sorrow in my heart all day?
How long will evil forces threaten to destroy me?

Consider, and answer me, O Lord God;
Lighten my eyes lest I sleep the sleep of death;
lest unscrupulous tycoons distort my values;
lest professional panderers delude me.

For I have trusted in your steadfast love;
I have kept my ears open to your voice
Even when those who oppose you clamored for my attention;
But the clamor is deafening! Let it cease for a while, Lord.
That I may draw strength from the quiet awareness of your presence.

But we who struggle to right the wrong must be content
To give ourselves fully and fondly, like Jesus Christ,
And believe in the resurrection
when only the evidence of death is visible.

Psalm 6

O Lord, there are those that say to you, "Reprove me not in your anger."
I cannot speak this way to you.
I cannot see you as a God of Wrath.
This, I think, is man's graven image fashioned out of the hard substance of his
own response to those who offend him.

I see you only as a God who invites us to trust and love.
In loving trust, I come to you, wet with the tears
that threaten to dim my eyes and heart.
It is not foes, but friends that have caused these tears to flow.
They think of effectiveness in terms of measured results.
They coldly computerize works whose essence transcends computation.
They place blocks of ice along the way where I walked with zeal and zest.
Save me, O Lord, from slipping.
Preserve me from fractured ideals, from the frostbite of blighted hopes.

I do not think that all is right with the world, Lord.
I know that much is very wrong.
But we who struggle to right the wrong must be content
To give ourselves fully and fondly, like Jesus Christ,
And believe in the Resurrection
when only the evidence of death is visible.

Vision of Concern

"The Lord has anointed me to bring good tidings to the afflicted; he has sent me to bind up the broken-hearted."

Is. 61:1

Share your joy with others, and you will find
that they have joy to share with you.

Psalm 4

Answer me when I call, O God of my right.
You have given me room when I was in distress.
Be gracious to me and hear my prayer.

Yahweh answers:
"Do not be deluded; do not be self-righteous.
Do not think yourself specially entitled to my help.
My desire is to protect all men, as yours should be.

Those who stray will not be set right by advice, but by loving concern.
Do not say the Lord has set apart the godly for himself.

Share your joy with others, and you will find that they have joy to share with you.
Share their burdens and you will find that they will shoulder yours.

Do not call me God of your right but call me the Great Integrator.

I will bring all men together in love, if they will liberate
themselves from their complacency, and explore the merits of others."

Yahweh, Great Integrator, you answered me when I called.
Your answer made me question myself and re-appraise others,
And look for you in them.

God meets me in the gardens and ghettos of the world,
and says, "You and I must build a bridge."

Psalm 11

In the Lord I take refuge.
How can you say to me:
"Flee like a bird to the mountains;
Barricade yourself in Suburbia,
And do not let the pollution of the
City rabble contaminate you."?

I reject your advice, and I repeat:
"In the Lord I take refuge."
Let me tell you what I mean by these words.

I do not mean flight;
I do not mean closing my eyes to hard
situations and hoping they will go away.

I mean risking the pain, the blame, the shame
That comes from involvement,
And believing that God somehow sustains me —
helps me to struggle in the dark and trust
that light will overtake the darkness;
helps me to sense his presence in the
interchange of people who need each other.

In God I take refuge — the God who
meets me in the ghettos and gardens of the world
and says to me: "You and I must build a bridge."

Men must be to men epiphanies of God.

Psalm 14

The fool says in his heart, "There is no God."
Should we denounce him?
Or should we not rather ask,
Am I responsible for the darkness that shrouds him?
For men must be to men epiphanies of God,
Reflecting wisdom and love;
Giving visible form to God's promise:
"I will be your God and you will be my people";
Bringing God to one another,
And one another to God,
By mutual fidelity and trust.
Forgive me, Lord, if I have denied you
by projecting false images of you.
For this is the greatest foolishness of all.
Beside it, the denial of the "fool" is a folly that saves —
saves man from accepting as God, man's inadequate projections.

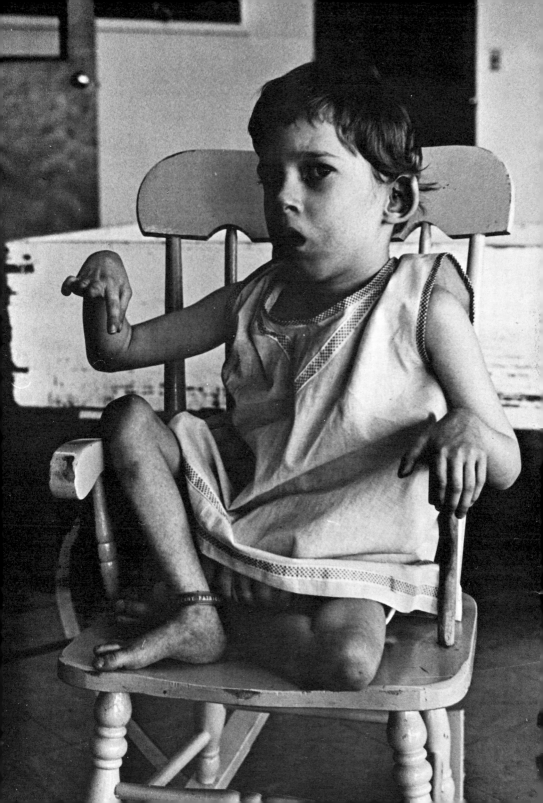

Sustain us by your enduring fidelity,
So that we may seek to support, not to control our brother.

Psalm 7

O Lord, my God, in you I take refuge;
Save me from my pursuers, but save my pursuers.
Draw them and me by your steadfast love,
So that we will not run from one another but toward one another.
Sustain us by your enduring fidelity,
So that we may seek to support, not to control our brother.
As once we dug pits to bury our rivals' talents
Let us now build halls of human endeavor with room to
accommodate man's diverse gifts.
Help us, Lord, to appreciate one another's uniqueness;
Help us to rejoice in the achievements of others,
And to invite them to rejoice in our own.
Help us to mobilize against the enemies within:
Jealousy and Hate;
Suspicion and Guile;
Frustration, Isolation, Boredom.
Arm us with your steadfast love, your flawless truth, your zest for life,
That we may build the earth which you have given us,
And remember while we build:
"Unless the Lord build the house they labor in vain that build."

In the glow of the ribbons of light,
In the verve of the dashing waves, let us find the strength
to enlighten and refresh all God's people.

Psalm 19

The heavens are telling the glory of God,
And the firmament proclaims his handiwork.
Ribbons of light stream across the sky,
And dashing waves break on the rock-ridged shore.

Tots and teens and "three-scores" feel at home here,
And the generation gap somehow is eliminated,
As each one looks about him and cries:
"Life can be beautiful!"

Life can be beautiful, Lord, if mankind does not pollute it.
Forgive us for the times we have failed to admit this,
For the times we have supplanted the ribbons of light with lurid streaks of hate;
For moments when we have been blind
to the light in our brother's eye and seen only the mote;
For occasions when we have fashioned into walls that divide
Rocks that could form the foundation to build a house of love.
The heavens are telling the glory of God,
And the firmament proclaims his handiwork.
In the glow of the ribbons of light,
In the verve of the dashing waves, let us find the strength
to enlighten and refresh all God's people.

My Gospel is disarmament; my message, love and peace.

Psalm 18

"I love Thee, O Lord, my strength.
The Lord is my rock, my fortress and my deliverer.
I call upon the Lord, who is worthy to be praised,
and I am saved from my enemies.
The Lord thundered from the heavens, and the Most High uttered His voice,
The Lord rewarded me according to my righteousness.
He trains my hands for war, so that my arm can bend a bow of bronze.

I pursued my enemies and overtook them.
I thrust them through so that they were not able to rise.
For thou didst girt me with strength for the battle.
I bent them fine as dust before the wind;
I cast them out like the mire of the streets."

Yahweh answers:
"You tell me that you love me but do you really know me?
You call me 'rock and fortress'.
You speak of me as 'thundering from the heavens';
As 'training your hands for war'.
This is not myself but some strange god whom you envision.
This is a god whom you have fashioned — a power-crazed idol whom you worship.
You boast of 'thrusting your enemies through,
so that they were not able to rise' ——— and
you give me credit for having girded
you with 'strength for the battle'.

Continued

48

Psalm 18

Permit me to disillusion you.
I arm no one with strength for battle.
My Gospel is disarmament; my message, love and peace.
You startle me when you say:
'The Lord rewarded me according to my righteousness' —
for such words reveal how unfamiliar
you are with my Covenant of Love.
Love does not reward; Love shares.
You grieve me when you say of your enemies:
'I beat them fine as dust before the wind;
I cast them out like the mire of the streets'.
Have you never learned respect for life?
respect for all mankind in whom I live, through whom I love?
You say, 'I love thee, O Lord,' and I answer, 'Do you know me?'
Look long and lovingly at all your fellow men,
And speak those words to them.
Love them, and help them to live fully and freely.
Then, and then only will I believe that you love me."

Vision of Hope

"There shall be heard again the voice of mirth and the voice of gladness, the voice of the bridegroom and the voice of the bride, the voices of those who sing as they bring thank offerings to the Lord."

Je. 33:11

I hear your voice inside of me.

Psalm 3

O Lord, how many are those who oppose me,
Those who look on my authentic response to renewal and say:
"There is no help for such a one in God."

But you give me strength to lift my head and smile.
I cry out to you in moments of prayer and you respond.

I hear your voice inside of me, and in the pleas and proposals of those I serve.

At coffee breaks and moments of leisure, I feel your presence.
I am not afraid, though thousands set themselves against me.

Answer me, O Lord!
Deliver me from the cult of uniformity
Which some would sacralize and eternalize.
Deliver me from those who condemn me
for recognizing you as the God of this evolving world.

Live life thoroughly enough to incite others
to cry out mightily, "Let's celebrate life!"

Psalm 12

Help, Lord, for there is no longer any that is godly;
for the faithful have vanished from among the sons of men.
Everyone utters lies to his neighbor.
With flattering lips and a double heart they speak.

Yahweh answers:
It is true that the faithful in great numbers have vanished.
It is true that lies and flattery abound,
but aren't you being shortsighted
when you say that no one is godly?
that everyone utters lies?
Look a little harder and you will find upright men.
Probe a little deeper and you will discover
that the liars and panderers would mend their ways
if they could experience an atmosphere of love.
Begin by believing in your own power to love and to be loved,
And take the risk of wagering that others will match the trust you place in them.
Believe, above all, that I am a God
Who invites all men to trust.
Do not think of me as one whom you fear,
but rather as someone who never stops believing in you,
never stops inviting you to look up and live.
Look up long enough to invite others to do likewise.
Live life thoroughly enough to incite others
to cry out mightily, "Let's celebrate life."

Love can triumph, fellowship can prevail
if we will but trust you and one another.

Psalm 10

Why do you seem so far away, Lord?
Why do you seem so silent when the poor are oppressed,
When the wicked grow rich by exploiting the poor,
When the powerful crowd you out of the world,
And proclaim in loud deeds,
"God is dead!"

For wickedness stamps through the world unmolested,
Robbing and killing and raping your people.
Wickedness laughs at the God-fearing,
Mocks those who proclaim the Gospel of Love.
"No need to save your fellow man," he says;
"God is dead! Love is dead!
Fight with might if you want to survive;
Mow down your foe before he destroys you.
Burn incense to Mars who inspires man to devise new nuclear weapons."

O God, I cannot accept his way of life.
Though his clamor makes it hard for me to hear your voice,
Though his pageantry hides you from my sight,
Something more perceptive than ears or eyes
Tells me that you are still with us,
That Love can triumph, that fellowship can prevail,
If we will but trust you and one another.

Flashes of your glory reach us
in little people and little things.

Psalm 8

Yahweh, my Lord, how excellent is your name in all the earth.
Your glory transcends us;
But flashes of it reach us in the splendor of the evolving universe,
And in little people and little things.

The beauty and magnitude of the heavens astound us:
The sun and moon; the whirling planets, and the scintillating stars.

What is man that you concern yourself with him?

Or the Son of Man?

Yahweh answers:
"Man is my image. He alone can reflect my love.
And the Son of Man has done this.
He is my Son in whom I am pleased.
He is your brother: he knows what man is;
He is your Saviour: he shows what man can be."

Yahweh, my Lord, how excellent is your name!
It speaks to us in the world you made:
In the mighty mountains and the surging seas;
But it comes alive in the Word Incarnate,
In Jesus Christ whose presence answers our question:
What is man? What is God?

May he support you in your efforts
to make the whole world his sanctuary, and every
human situation a shekinah.

Psalm 20

The Lord uphold you in the daily conflict!
The name of the God of love sustain you!
May he support you in your efforts to make the whole world his sanctuary,
And every human situation a shekinah.

May his presence encourage you in your new style of worship
Which is rooted in spirit and in truth,
And finds expression in existential holocausts:
Reparation, reconciliation, reverence for life.

May you be a militant in your concern for the rights of others,
But a pacifist in your loving acceptance of all men,
Whatever their creed, whatever their color, whatever their culture.
May you be as liberal as Yahweh who "lets all men be,"
And helps them to discover that no one can fully be
if he isolates himself from his fellow man.

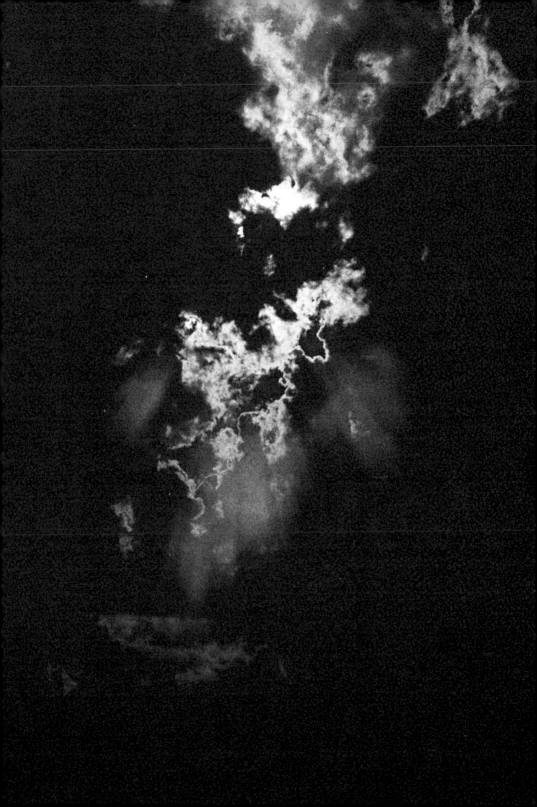